for 1000+ tutorials ... use our
free site .... drawinghowtodraw.com

BY RACHEL GOLDSTEIN

DRAWING FOR KIDS

WITH lowercase ALPHABET LETTERS IN EASY STEPS

CARTOONING FOR KIDS AND LEARNING HOW TO DRAW WITH THE LOWERCASE ALPHABET

LETTER A TURTLE

1.

2.

3.

4.

5.

6.

7.

#3 Shapes

↓ NOW YOU TRY ↓

LETTER B KOALA

1.

2.

3.

4.

5.

Letter C Shape

6.

7.

↓ NOW YOU TRY ↓

LETTER C HEDGEHOG

1.

2.

3.

4.

#3 Shape

5.

6.

#3 Shapes

Letter U
Fingers

↓ NOW YOU TRY ↓

LETTER D KITTY

1.

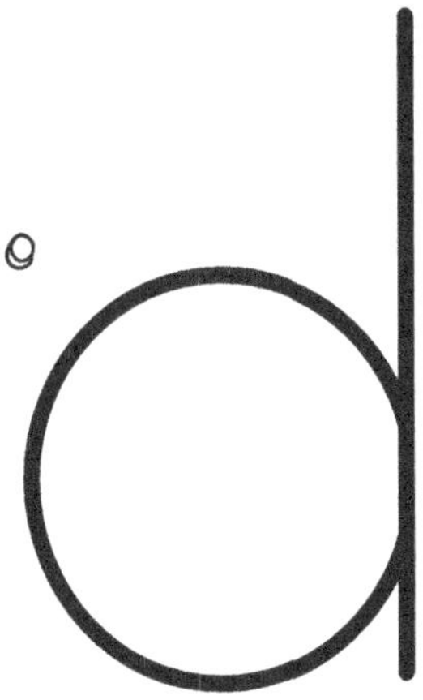

2. Letter b

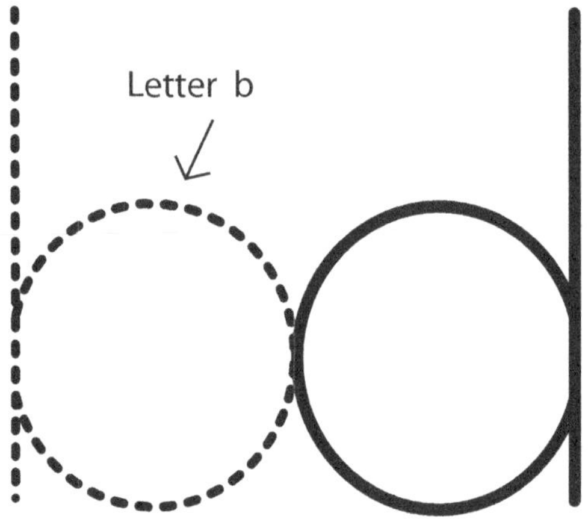

3.

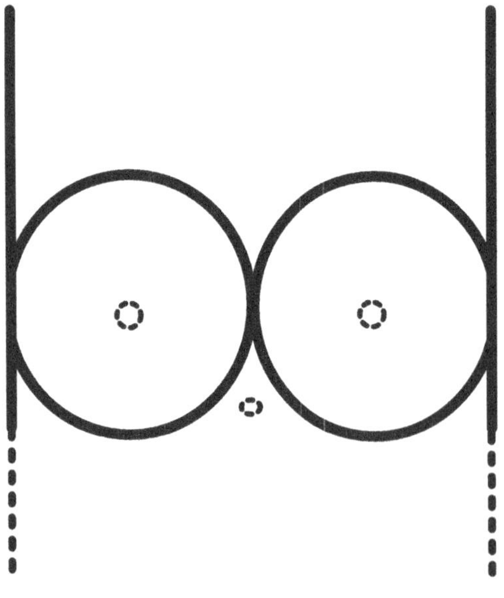

4. #3 Shape

5.

6.

NOW ⇒ YOU ⇒ TRY

LETTER E BORED BOY

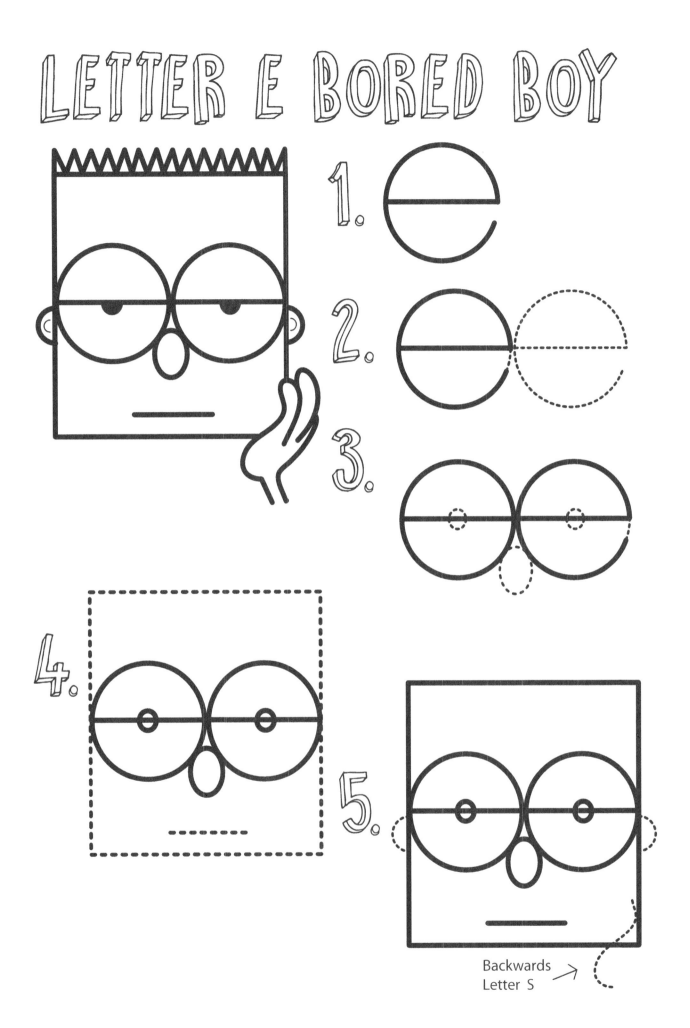

1.

2.

3.

4.

5.

Backwards → Letter S

6.

Backwards
Letter C
Shape

7.

8.

Letter L
Shape

↓ NOW YOU TRY ↓

LETTER F GIRAFFE

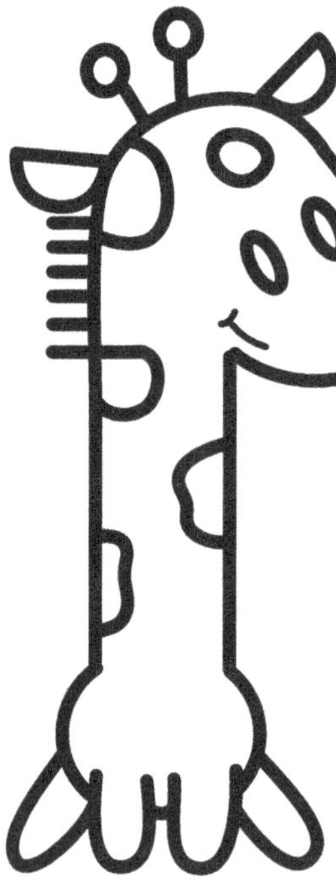

1.

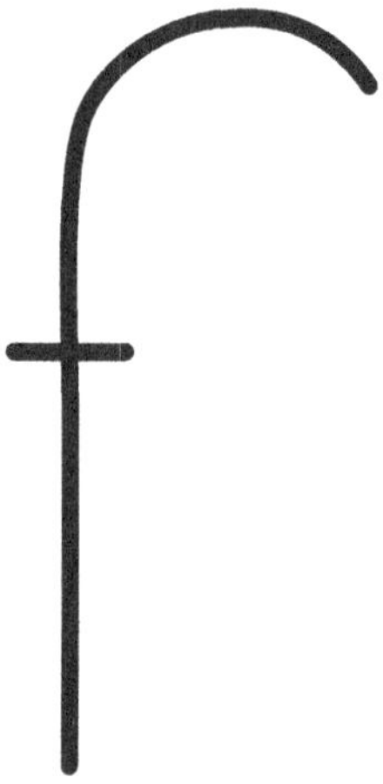

2. Letter J Shape

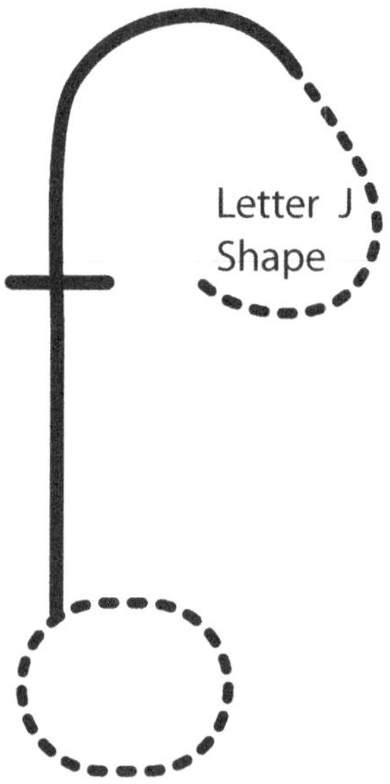

3. Letter D Shaped Ears

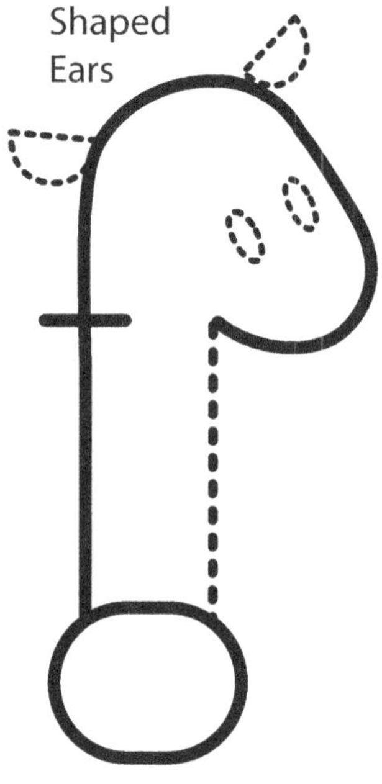

4. Letter U Legs

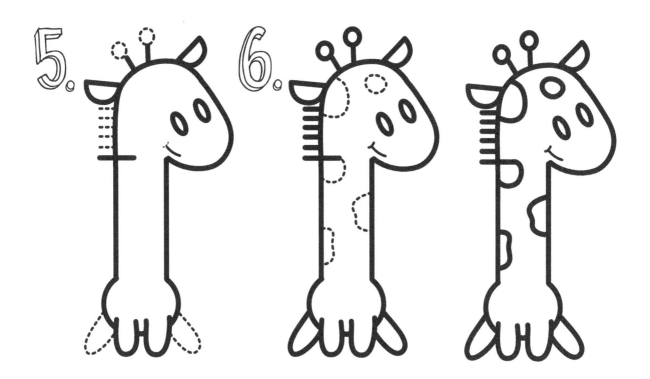

NOW YOU TRY

LETTER G GOAT

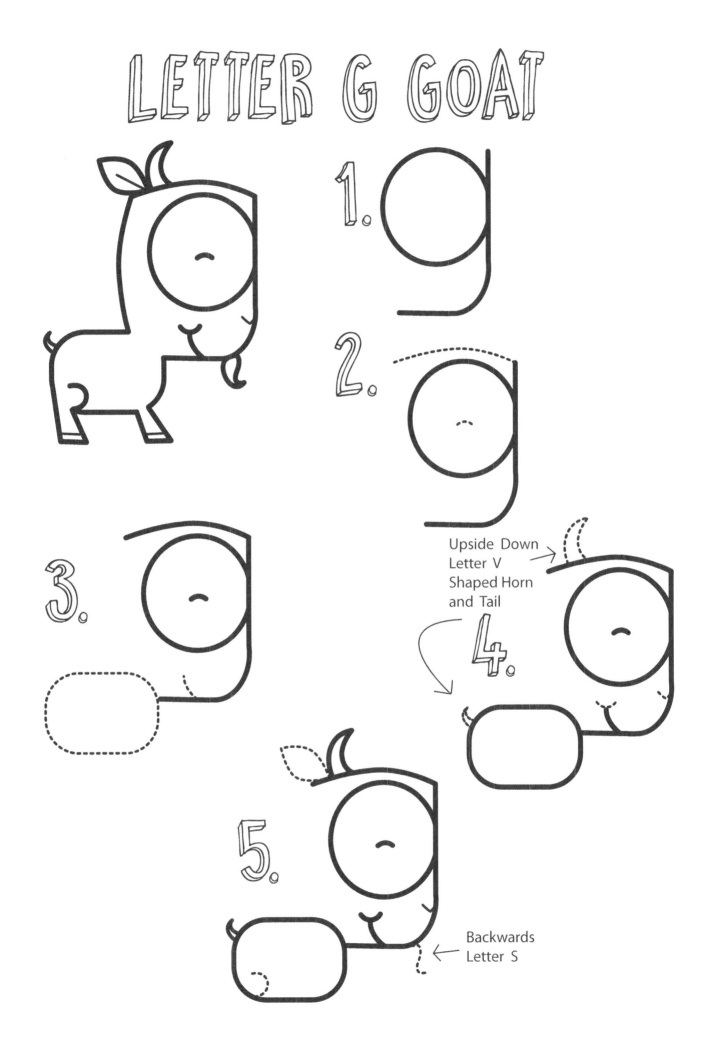

1.

2.

3.

4.
Upside Down
Letter V
Shaped Horn
and Tail

5.
Backwards
Letter S

LETTER H DOGGY

1.

2.

3.

4. Letter V Shapes

5.

6.

7.

8.

Letter U Tongue

Letter
V
Tail

↓ NOW YOU TRY ↓

LETTER I DOLPHIN

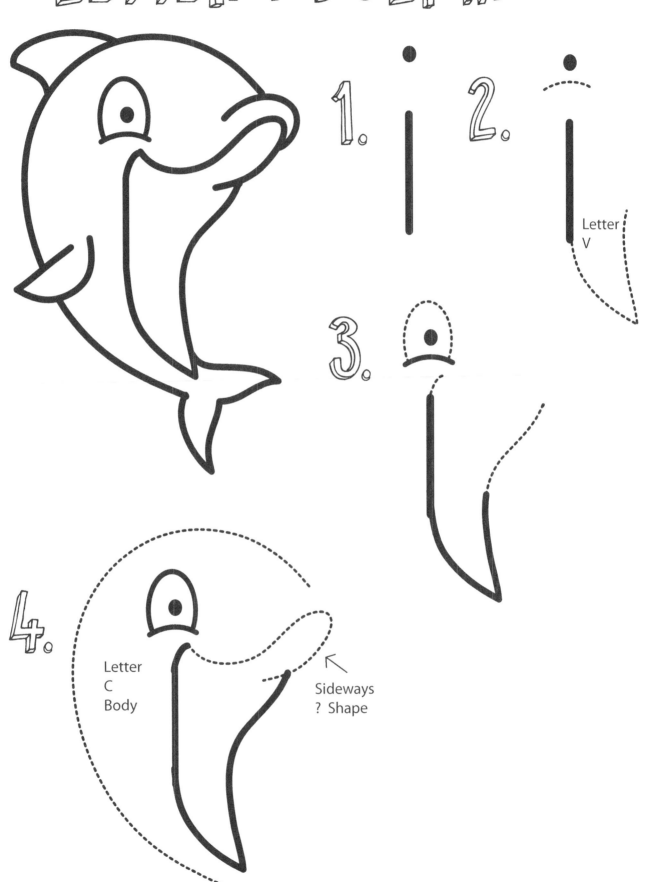

1.

2.

Letter
V

3.

4.

Letter
C
Body

Sideways
? Shape

5.

Letter
D → Shape

← Letter
V Shape

6.

NOW YOU TRY!

LETTER J HORSEY

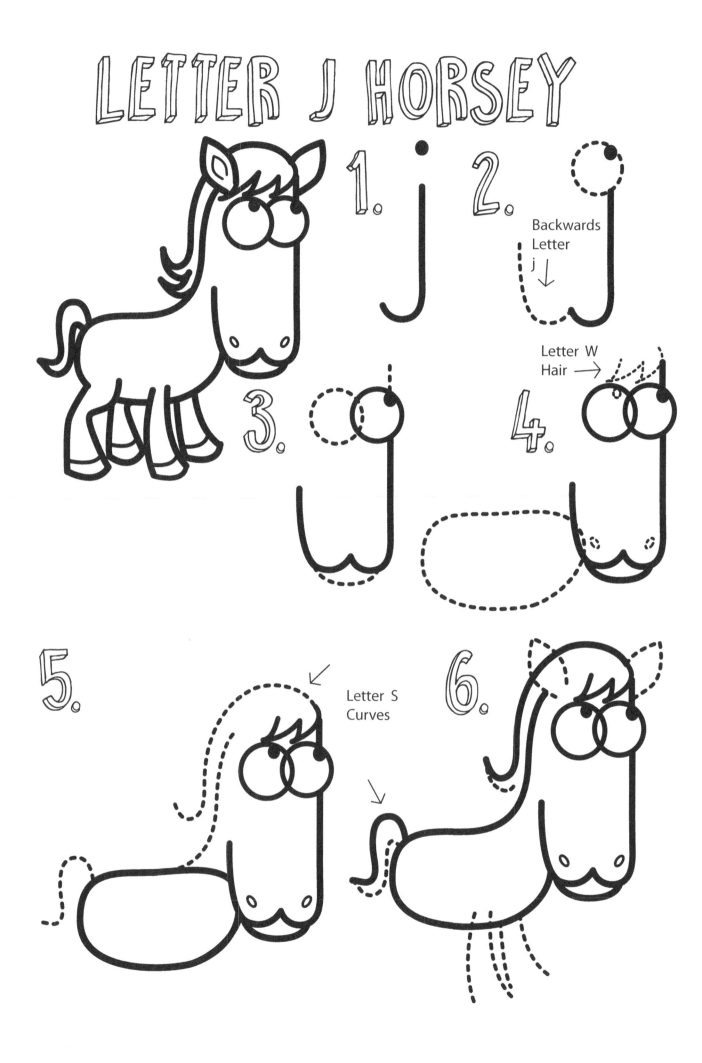

1. j

2. Backwards Letter j ↓

3.

4. Letter W Hair →

5. Letter S Curves

6.

7.

Letter V Shape

? Shape

8.

9.

↓ NOW YOU TRY ↓

LETTER K CHICKEN

1.

2.

3.

4.

5.

#3
Shapes

6.

#3

Letter J wings

7. 8.

#3 Shapes

↓ NOW YOU TRY ↓

LETTER L BIRD IN TREE

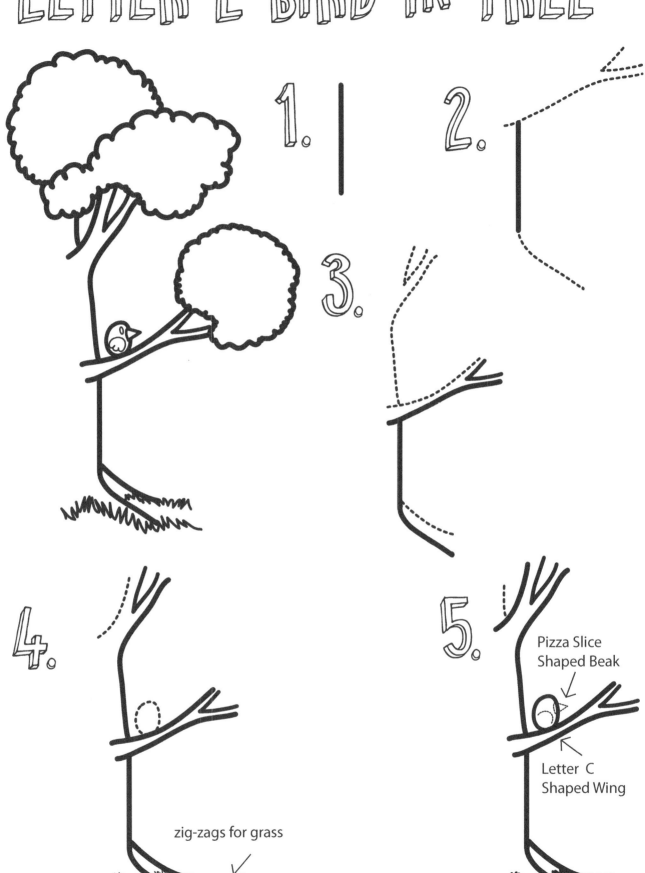

1.

2.

3.

4.

zig-zags for grass

5.

Pizza Slice Shaped Beak

Letter C Shaped Wing

Clouds for Tops of Trees

6.

#3 Shape on Wing

7.

Finish Wing with a Curved Line

↓ NOW YOU TRY ↓

LETTER M MONKEY

1. m 2. m

3. 4. #3 Shape

5. #3 Tongue

6. Letter U Shapes

7.

8. Letter S Curve on Each Hand   #3 and Letter C Shapes

9. Letter C, J, and U Shapes

10.

#8 on Each Hand

↓ NOW YOU TRY ↓

LETTER N STUDENT

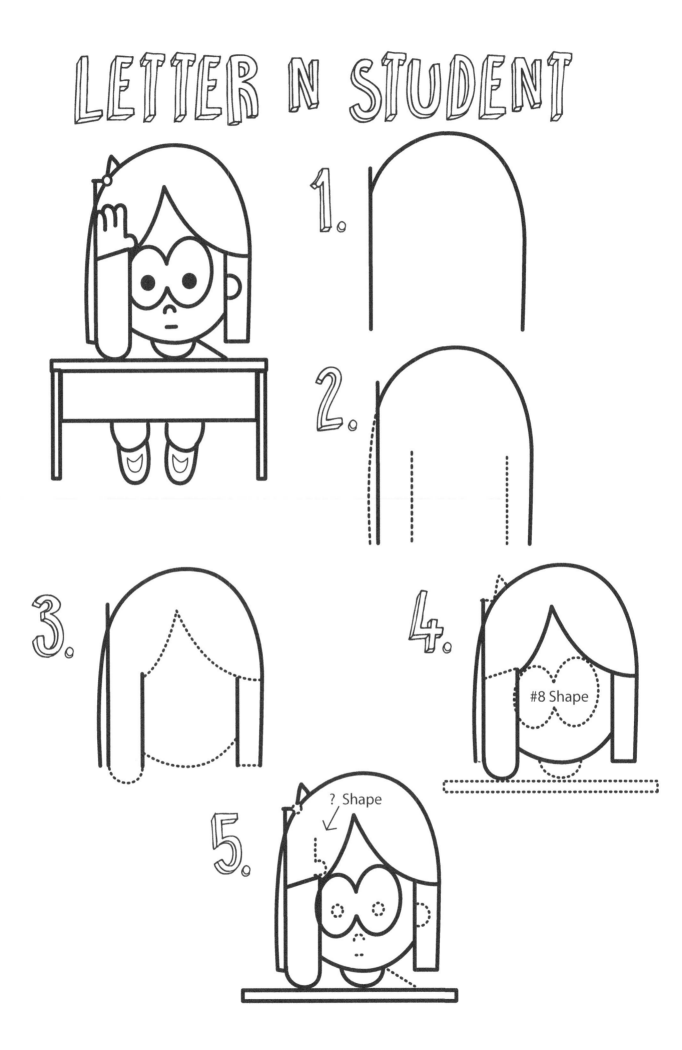

1.

2.

3.

4. #8 Shape

5. ? Shape

6.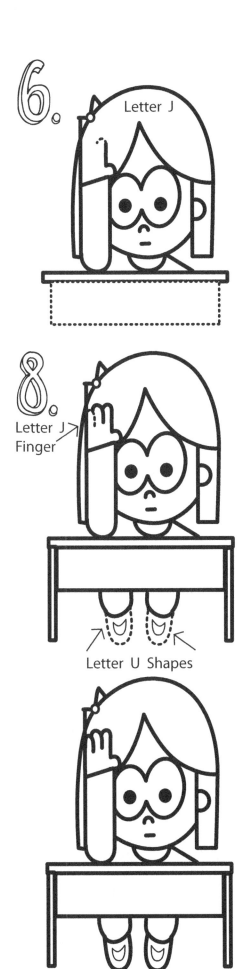

Letter J

7.
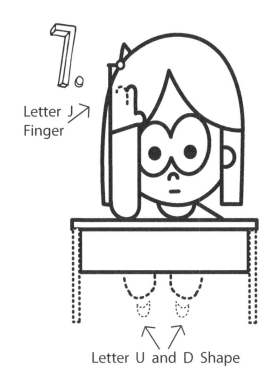

Letter J ↗
Finger

Letter U and D Shape

8.
Letter J ↗
Finger

Letter U Shapes

↓ NOW YOU TRY ↓

LETTER O PENGUIN

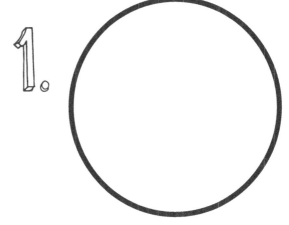

1.

2.

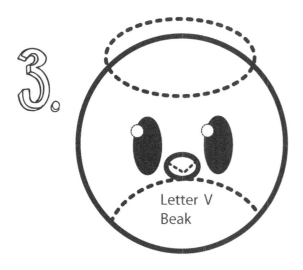

3.

Letter V
Beak

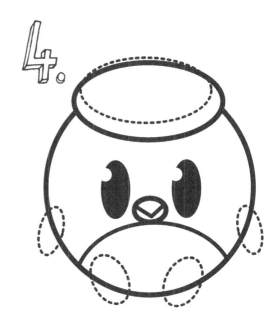

4.

5.

6.

Cloud Shape

⇓ NOW YOU TRY ⇓

LETTER P BIRD IN TREE

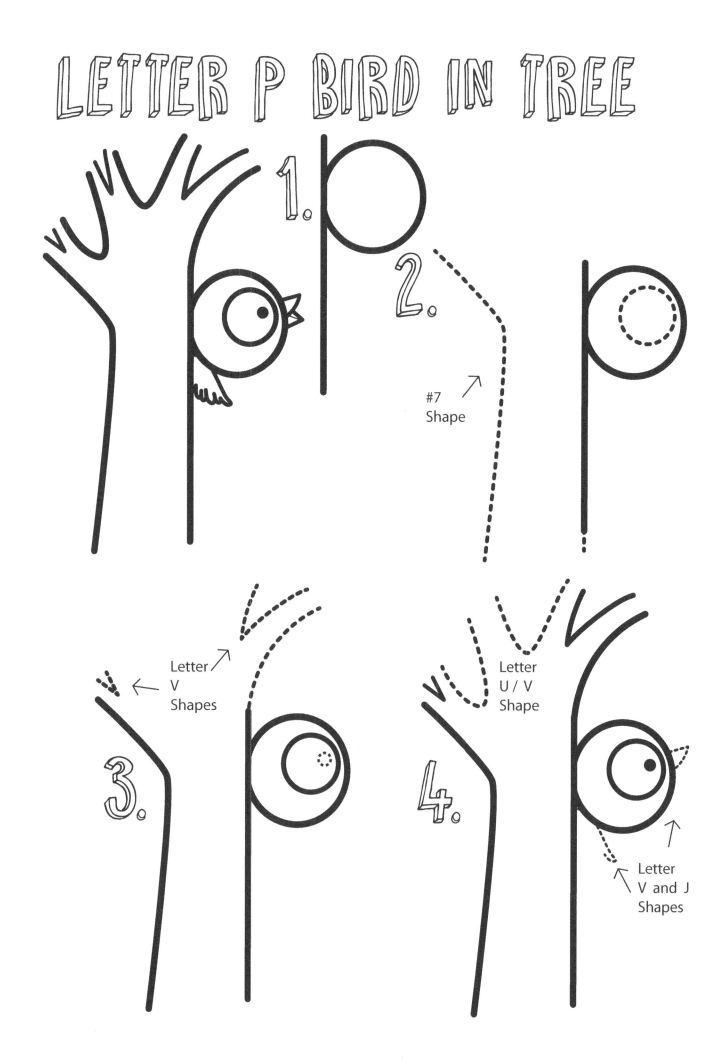

1.

2.

#7 Shape

Letter V Shapes

Letter U / V Shape

3.

4.

Letter V and J Shapes

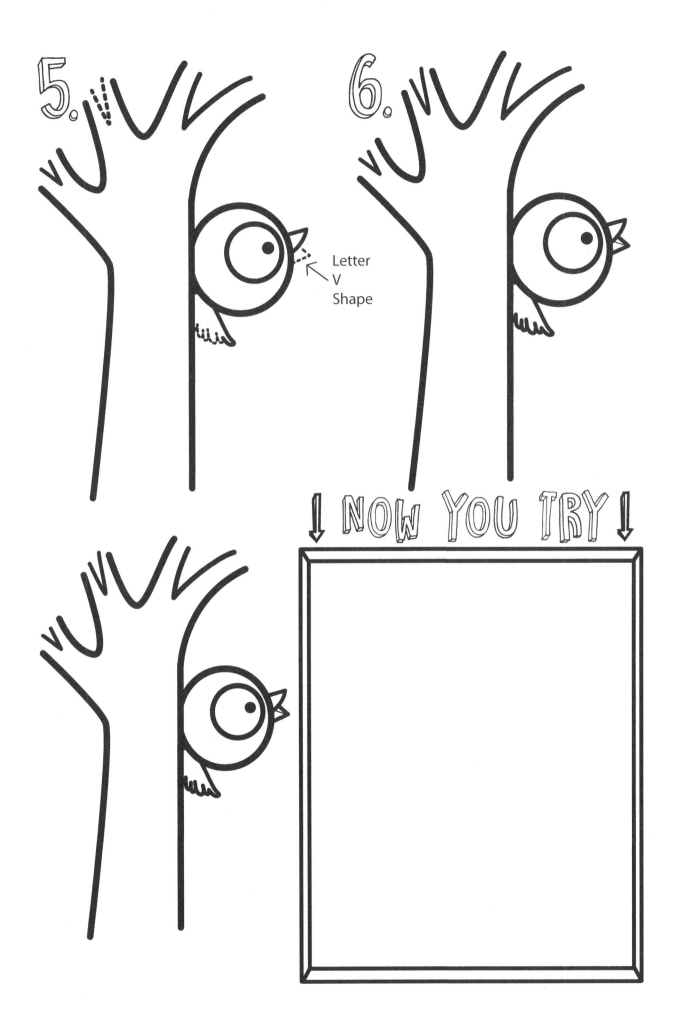

5.

Letter
V
Shape

6.

↓ NOW YOU TRY ↓

LETTER Q ANGRY MAN

1.

2.

3.

4.

LETTER R SILLY COW

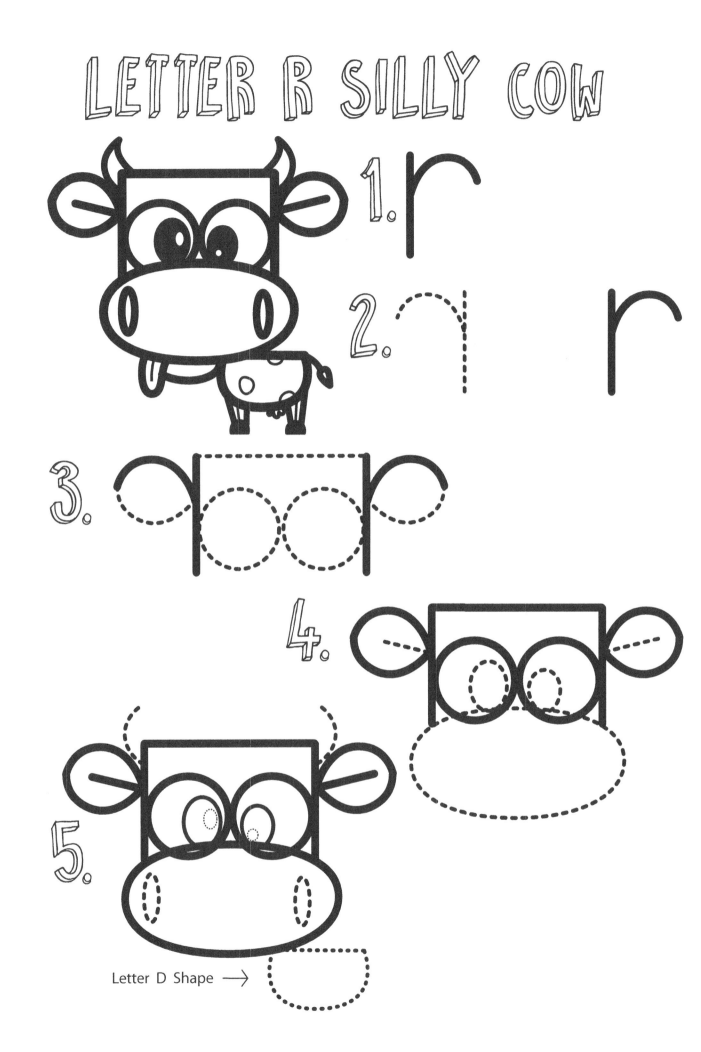

1. r

2. r

3.

4.

5.

Letter D Shape →

LETTER S SWAN

1.

2.

#8 Shape

#3 Shape

3.

#2 Shape

4.

5.

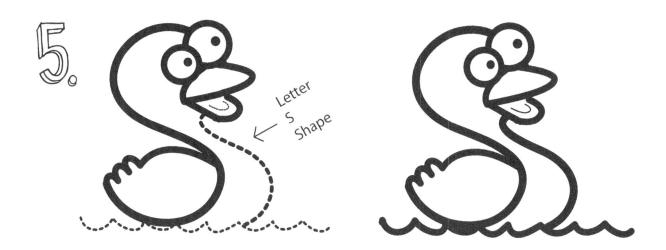

Letter S Shape

↓ NOW YOU TRY ↓

LETTER T TEETHY GIRL

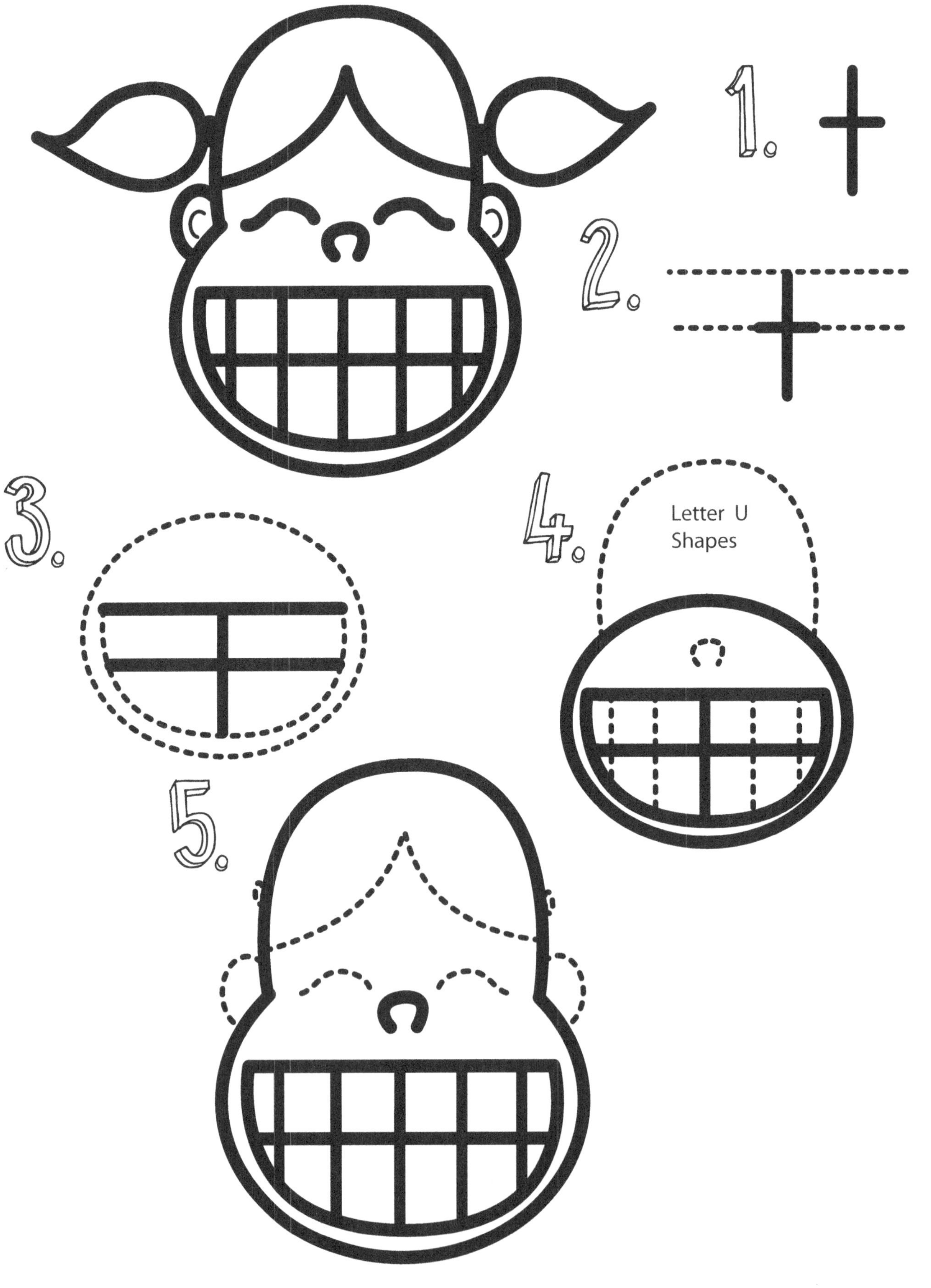

1. +

2. ⊹ (dotted cross between dashed lines)

3. (dotted circle with T shape)

4. Letter U Shapes

5.

6. Letter C Shapes

7. Letter V Shapes

↓ NOW YOU TRY ↓

LETTER U BUNNY

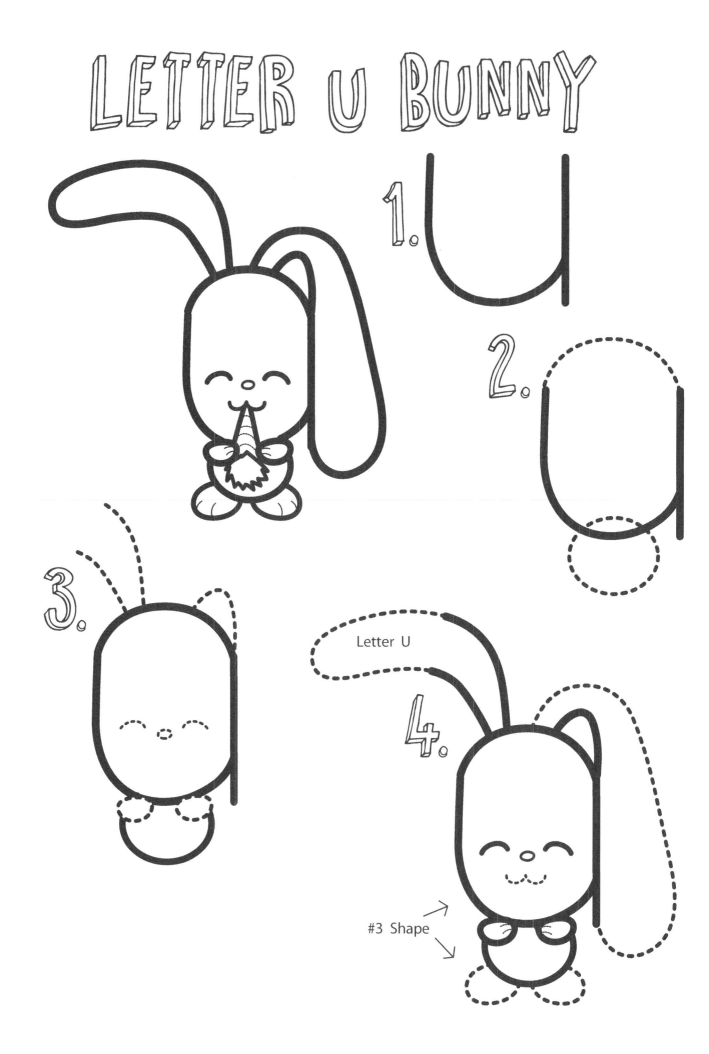

1.

2.

3.

4.

Letter U

#3 Shape

5.

6.

↓ NOW YOU TRY ↓

LETTER V BIRD ON BRANCH

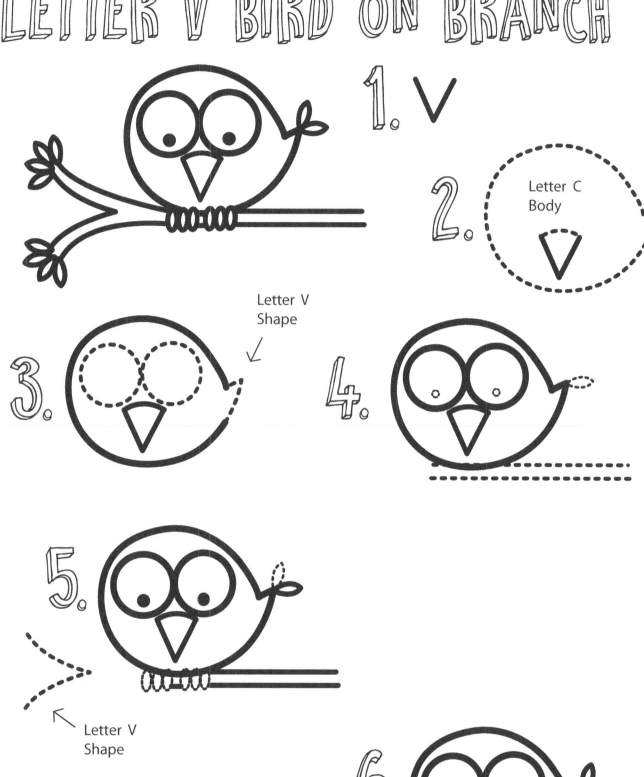

1. V

2. Letter C Body

3.

Letter V Shape

4.

5. Letter V Shape

6.

1.

NOW YOU TRY

LETTER W WORKING MAN

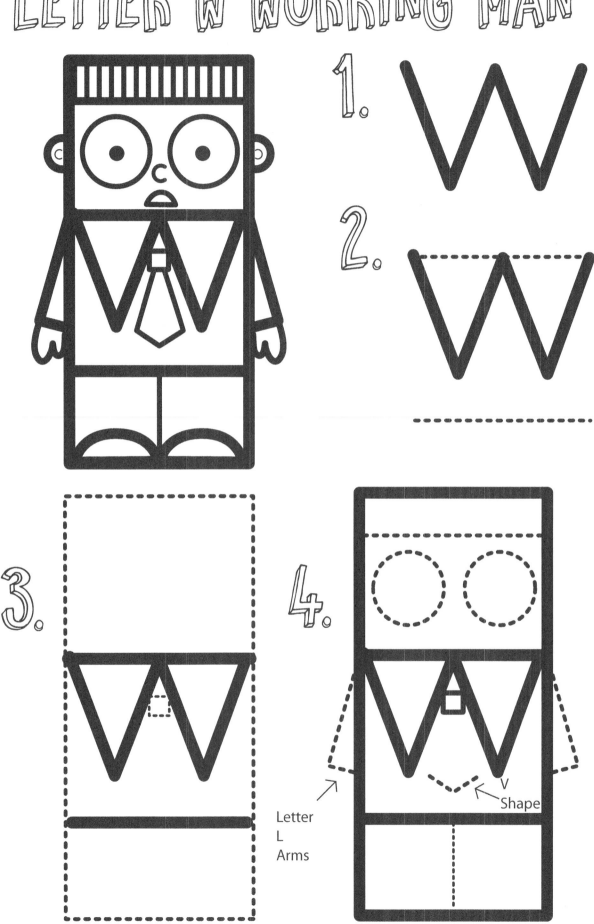

1.

2.

3.

4.

Letter
L
Arms

V
Shape

5.

← Letter D Mouth

6.

#3 Hands

Letter B Shoes

↓ NOW YOU TRY ↓

LETTER X KISSING BEARS

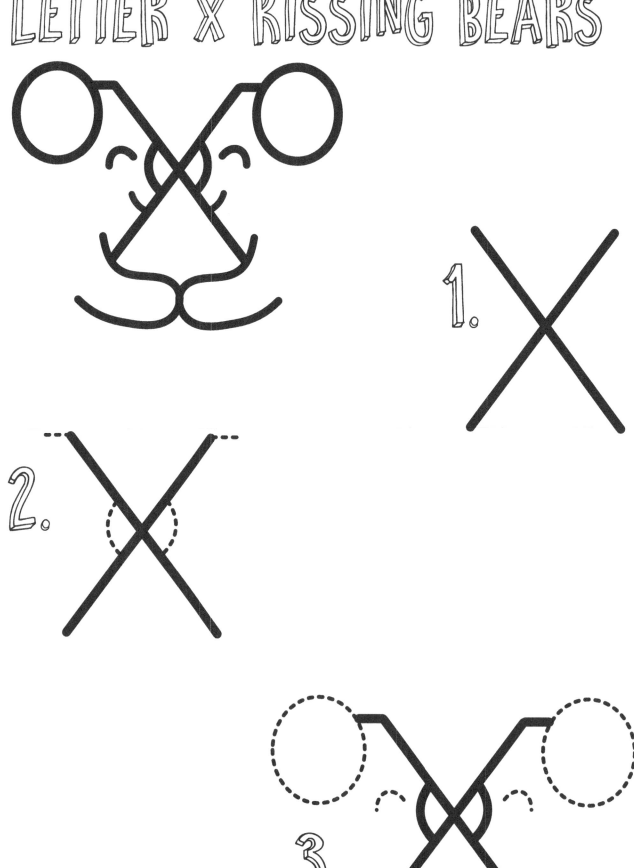

1.

2.

3.

4.

↓ NOW YOU TRY ↓

LETTER Y POSSUM

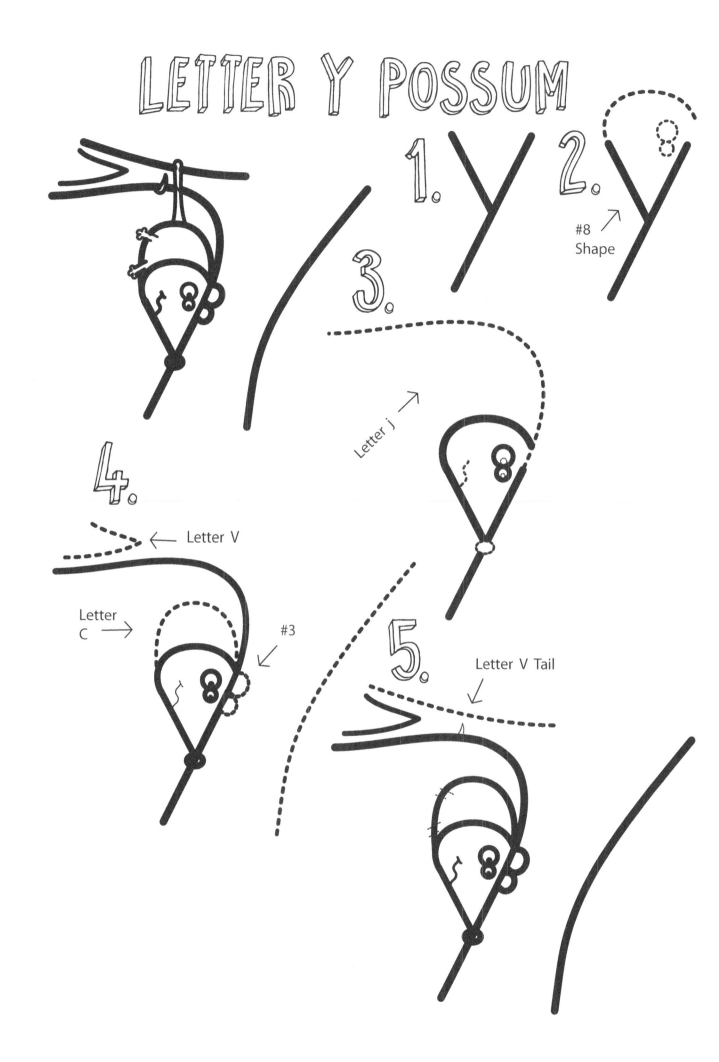

1.

2. #8 Shape

3. Letter j

4. Letter V
Letter C
#3

5. Letter V Tail

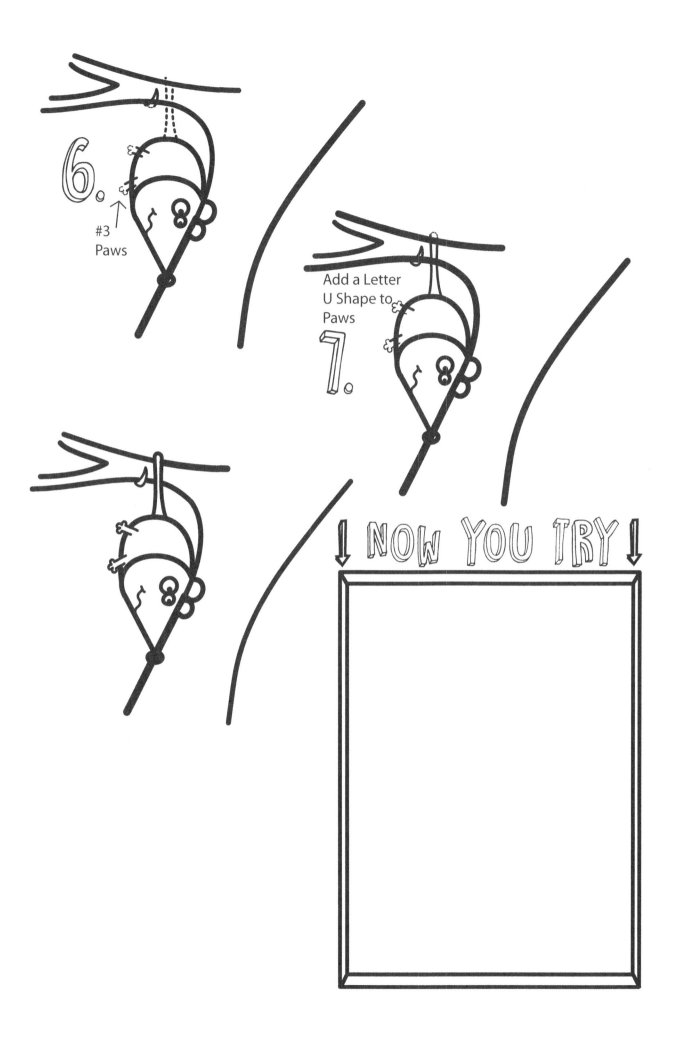

6.

#3
Paws

7.

Add a Letter
U Shape to
Paws

↓ NOW YOU TRY ↓

LETTER Z DUCKY

1. Z

2. Z

3.

4.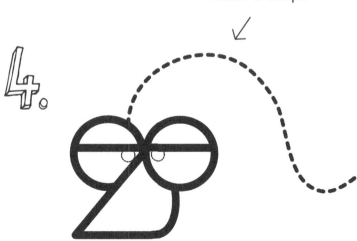

Letter S Shape

5.

6.

Letter C Wing

↓ NOW YOU TRY ↓

Made in the USA
Las Vegas, NV
25 November 2023